A
Guide to
Tune Analysis
and
Chord/Scale Choices
for
Improvisation

By DAN HAERLE

HAL•LEONARD®
CORPORATION

7777 W. BLUEMOUND RD. P.O. BOX 13819 MILWAUKEE, WI 53213

Dedicated to Jack Petersen, a dear friend and one of my best teachers.

Thanks to my friends, Jamey Aebersold, David Baker, Jerry Coker, Matt Nicholl, Mike Steinel, Jack Petersen and David Joyner for their helpful suggestions.

Editing and design
consulting: Jill Haerle

Produced by Dan Haerle on an
Apple™ Macintosh Plus computer
using:

Ready, Set Go!™
Letraset USA
40 Eisenhower Drive
Paramus, NJ 07653

NoteWriter™
Passport Designs, Inc.
625 Miramontes St.
Half Moon Bay, CA USA 94019

Sonata™ font
Adobe Systems Incorporated
1585 Charleston Road
Mountain View, CA 94039

Copyright © 1989 HAL LEONARD PUBLISHING CORPORATION
International Copyright Secured   ALL RIGHTS RESERVED   Printed in the U.S.A.
For all works contained herein:
Unauthorized copying, arranging, adapting, recording or public performance is an infringement of copyright.
Infringers are liable under the law.

Table of Contents ─────────────────────

Foreword

Once again Dan Haerle has discovered a void in jazz education materials and has moved to fill it. The Jazz Sound, despite its modest and unassuming title, is much more than just another chord/scale book. It is the first such work to move beyond the dissemination of basic information regarding chord/scale relationships to address such crucial concerns as how understanding a composition influences our scale choices beyond the obvious and how melody, function and context play a major role in determining the best possible scale to be used in a given situation. The excellent summaries and the chapter on bracketing alone justify the purchase of this book.

The Jazz Sound is not only revolutionary in concept but is also informative, concise, comprehensive and well-organized. It is a valuable and welcome addition to the growing body of teaching materials.

David Baker
Distinguished Professor of Music
Chairman of the Jazz Department
Indiana University School of Music

Introduction

The main thrust of this book is to help musicians develop a way of thinking about the music they play. The concepts presented will enable you to choose the right sounds for the chord progressions you wish to use as vehicles for improvisation. The book can serve as a resource to take directly to the music as you strive to accomplish a realization of the printed page.

As the art of improvisation has become more sophisticated, the challenge of treating complex music appropriately has become, at times, a formidable one. Improvisors must often look beyond the obvious chord/scale relationships to understand nuances of the music which the composer has indicated in subtle ways. It isn't adequate to simply play right notes if they aren't really suggested by the "flow" of the piece. Just as anyone can hear a "clam" or wrong note, so it is also obvious that one set of tones sounds more natural in a given context than another. You have only to listen to become aware of the wonderful system of order which exists quite naturally in the musical universe.

Some chord/scale relationships are "cut and dried"; that is, certain notes must be present in the scale to supply the specified extensions or alterations of the chord. The improvisor must codify and recognize such situations and simply deal with them without any agonizing over a personal opinion.

An improvisor is responsible to the composer just as a performer is responsible to the composer of a classical work. Whether it was conceived consciously or unconsciously, the composer definitely created an aura around his piece which is a subtle combination of the melody, the chord symbols and the chord progression itself as well as the rhythmic style. To attempt to make appropriate chord/scale choices based only on chord symbols means seeing only the "tip of the iceberg."

Music is not a static art; it is sound occurring over a period of time. Therefore, each chord symbol cannot be considered separately. The improvisor, as an artist, must get in touch with the entire composition and get beneath the surface of the obvious suggestions of chord symbols. Getting the right general type of chord/scale isn't enough. You must take extra steps to get the right jazz sound!

Chapter 1 - Understanding a Composition ————

The first goal in preparing a vehicle for improvisation is to try to understand what the piece "sounds like." There's a distinction to be made here which is the difference between fact and opinion. Before you exercise your opinions in any field of endeavor, it's essential to know the facts. In a composition, the facts are the basic sounds that are the inherent nature of the piece and the opinions are the creative options (chord/scale choices) which are available. Understanding the facts implies several things which can be summarized as follows:

1) What are the key areas of the piece?
2) What are the specifics of the chord symbols?
3) What are the implications of the melody?
4) What tones are shared by chord/scales?

1) What are the key areas of the piece?

The piece might have one key area for the whole tune but usually there are two or more keys, for example, a major key and its relative minor. The following example is such a progression bracketed into key areas:

Many compositions modulate frequently and include more than two or three key areas. The following chord progression is typical of many tunes of the '50s and '60s:

C Major   Eb Major   D Major

| C △ | F mi7   Bb 7 | Eb △ | E mi7   A 7 |

Db Major   A Major

| Eb mi7   Ab 7 | Db △ | B mi7   E 7 | A △ |

2) What are the specifics of the chord symbols?

If a chord progression includes only triads and 7th chords lacking alterations, then this step may not be necessary. That is, the chord symbols may not reveal information other than what the basic chord groups are. The next example is typical of many chord progressions from the '20s, '30s and '40s which were quite simple in structure:

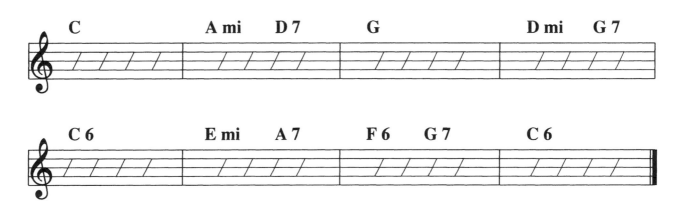

| C | A mi   D 7 | G | D mi   G 7 |

| C 6 | E mi   A 7 | F 6   G 7 | C 6 |

However, many pieces contain chord symbols which are quite specific and which represent subtle variations of chords of the same family. The next example is a progression which is typical of the '50s and '60s:

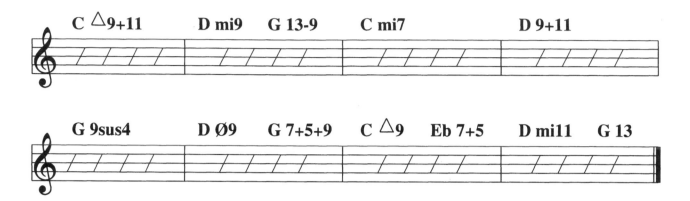

3) What are the implications of the melody?

In older tunes, composers often wrote colorful melodies which contained extensions or alterations of the harmony that weren't really described in the chord symbols. Possibly, it seemed unnecessary or redundant to do so or they simply didn't view harmony as altered or extended. The unfortunate thing is that the player, in his enthusiasm for improvising on simple chord symbols, sometimes disregards these subtleties and makes choices that don't reflect the sound of the melody. The following example shows a melodic line with the implied alterations or extensions shown in parentheses:

If the melody is ignored and the chord/scales chosen are based strictly on the chord symbols, the resulting improvisation can sound very different from the original composition. This suggests a very good question: If you don't want your improvisation to sound like the composition, why do you choose to play the piece? It might be better if you wrote your own piece with a similar but different sound.

There are many examples of similar kinds of chord progressions

If you don't want your improvisation to sound like the composition, why do you choose to play the piece?

such as blues tunes, "I Got Rhythm" tunes, originals based on the chords of standards, etc. An improvisor must be sensitive to differences that are often only suggested by the tune or the melody.

The next example shows a blues progression in the key of F. The tune strongly suggests +9 alterations on the I chords, a +11 alteration on the IV chord and a +5 alteration on the V chord:

4) What tones are shared by chord/scales?

Human beings are creatures of habit and are often comfortable with things staying the same. We've all heard the saying, "Don't rock the boat." While maintaining the status quo may be a cop out, sometimes that's a good rule to obey musically. If certain tones that we've been hearing can naturally continue into the next chord/scale, our ears are comfortable letting them. This tends to create a relaxed effect in the music. Also, being aware of this relationship allows us to make unexpected musical choices which create pleasant surprises in the sound as well. However, the starting point must be to understand the smoothest flow with the fewest number of changes which, I believe, is the natural tendency of the piece.

> *If certain tones that we've been hearing can naturally continue into the next chord/scale, our ears are comfortable letting them.*

The following example shows a chord progression which is satisfied with the simplest and fewest number of scales possible:

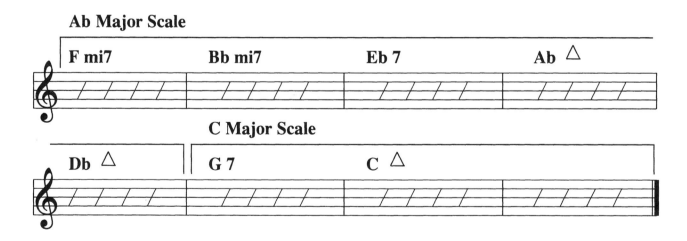

Once you have arrived at an understanding of the simplest nature of a particular piece, then you are prepared to either treat it that way or to choose surprising options which may add variety and excitement.

It should be mentioned that to deal successfully with a piece, you must have an accurate lead sheet of it. Many jazz pieces may only be found in illegal "fake" books which often contain inaccuracies in terms of both melody notes and chord symbols. Also, many compositions are not even available in print, and may have to be transcribed from a recording. In either case, it's a good idea to listen to several recordings of the same piece and consult another musician whose ability to hear chords and melody notes has been proven.

There are more legal books of jazz tunes becoming available now and these tend to be quite accurate. Another good source of lead sheets is the Jamey Aebersold play-along record series. This series offers collections of tunes by famous jazz composers. The books, which go with the records, contain lead sheets to the tunes that have been supplied either by the composers themselves or the publishers of their music.

In any case, you must carefully learn both the melody and the chords to the piece you want to use as a vehicle for improvisation. Or else, you have done a disservice to the composer before you even begin improvising on his composition.

The following questions form the basis of a complete concept of tune analysis which will serve you well in arriving at the true nature of the sound of a piece in an objective manner.

Summary:

Questions which help in understanding a composition:

1) What are the key areas of the piece?

2) What are the specifics of the chord symbols?

3) What are the implications of the melody?

4) What tones are shared by chord/scales?

Chapter 2 - Set Chord/Scale Relationships ————————

Certain chord/scale relationships aren't really open to personal opinion. In fact, it's very difficult to separate the chord from the scale at all because, often, they contain the same exact notes in a different arrangement. Take, for example, a minor 13th chord which contains the same seven notes as a Dorian scale on the same root:

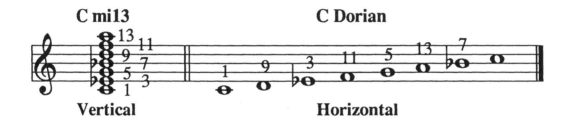

In this case, notice that Dorian doesn't just relate to a minor 13th, it <u>is</u> a minor 13th written out in a horizontal arrangement instead of a vertical arrangement. If there are no alterations specified in the chord symbol or implied by the melody, then the choice is "cut and dried." Such relationships are "set" and are summarized in this chapter.

In tune analysis, you don't need to agonize over set chord/scales but simply need to have a thorough knowledge of them and be able to recognize when they are called for. The summary that follows can be a quick mini-reference within this book for recalling the proper sound for certain specific types of chords.

The scales included here are the common scale forms only and don't include any synthetic scale forms. Since the improvisor must react to chord symbols with a scale choice, the set relationships are summarized by chord family. In Appendix II, an example of each chord/scale may be found.

Set Chord/Scales

Major Chord Family	Scale Choice
Maj 7sus4	Ionian
Maj 7 +11	Lydian
Maj 13	Lydian

Minor Chord Family	Scale Choice
Min 13	Dorian
Min 9 -5	Locrian, #2

Dominant Chord Family	Scale Choice
Dom 7sus4	Mixolydian
Dom 13	Lydian, b7
Dom 7 +5	Whole Tone
Dom 7 +11	Lydian, b7
Dom 13-9	Half-Whole Diminished
Dom 7-9-13	5th Mode of Harmonic Minor
Dom 7+5 +9	Super Locrian
Dom 9-13	Mixolydian, b6

Chapter 3 - Bracketing Chord Changes

Our musical tradition is based on a major/minor key system and, whether we realize it or not, we're all conditioned to relate what we hear to key areas. Compared with some forms of "brainwashing," this is a normal type of orientation that we all share in common because of our upbringing.

When the tonalities are clearly delineated for us, we have a strong sense of the form and direction of a piece. Sometimes, we may wish to obscure some tonalities or slightly cloud their clarity to veil them in mystery and add intrigue to the composition. Nevertheless, the first priority should be to have the skill to make the key areas clear to the listener, if we wish to do so.

When you've recognized the key areas of a piece, you've also paved the way for the bracketing of groups of two or more chords with single scales. This can make the task of improvising over a chord progression easier since a new unique set of tones isn't needed for every successive chord. Moreover, bracketing produces the strongest sense of the tonalities of a piece since it generally implies using the major or minor scale of a particular tonality or key area.

Bracketing keys is the simplest approach to chord/scale relationships, since the result is the fewest possible number of keys implied (and scales used). Using separate scales for each sound in a chord

Using a simple approach doesn't mean it's bad, nor does a complex approach mean it's good.

progression is a complex approach which essentially implies a different key for every chord. Using a simple approach doesn't mean it's bad, nor does a complex approach mean it's good. A simple approach may be what's needed to produce a smooth, relaxed musical effect whereas a complex approach may be needed to produce more tension. A skillful improvisor should have either of the approaches available to him. In the examples which follow, separate scales could be used for each of the chords. They haven't been chosen since the goal here is an understanding of bracketing.

The first examples show the two common ways of bracketing the II-V-I progressions in either major or minor. Since these progressions are cadences which establish the key areas, the use of the scales of the keys is the strongest way to sound the tonalities. This implies the use of the major scale of the key with a II-V-I in major and the harmonic minor scale of the key with a II-V-I in minor.

The following example uses only the tones of an F major scale over the entire progression:

The next example uses only the tones of a C harmonic minor scale over the entire progression. Notice the leading tone, B natural:

One thing should be mentioned regarding the preceding examples: Care must always be taken as to which tones are stressed in relation to any chord. Bracketing two or more chords with a single scale doesn't eliminate the need for a careful choice of notes. Important color tones such as 3rd's, 7th's and other extensions and alterations are generally going to need to be stressed. The bracketing of the progression is primarily for these two reasons:

1) To strengthen the tonality.

2) To simplify the problems of improvising on the progression.

The blues scales are so named because they lend themselves to bracketing most blues progressions. Though too much use of this type of bracketing could easily produce a monotonous effect, much of the blues tradition shows this type of approach to improvisation.

The following example shows the use of a "major" blues scale (1, 2, #2, 3, 5, & 6 of a major scale) over the entire progression.

In the previous excerpt, notice that only the six tones of a C major blues scale have been used. This is an extreme example and is quite repetitious, but it does demonstrate the flexible ability of the scale to work with all the chords in the progression. In actual practice, this blues scale would probably be used with other dominant 7th scales.

The next example shows the minor blues scale (1, b3, 4, #4, 5 & b7 of a major scale) used over the entire progression. Notice that only six tones are used in the entire chorus. Some care must be taken to avoid certain tones of the scale with certain chords.

As before, this example uses the C minor blues scale exclusively and, naturally, there's much repetition. Normally, you would probably use only fragments of the scale along with other dominant 7th scales for variety.

Tunes that primarily involve chords of one key may be effectively bracketed using the least number of scales. The next examples show the first eight bars of two common chord progressions. Both of these progressions can be bracketed with only two scales:

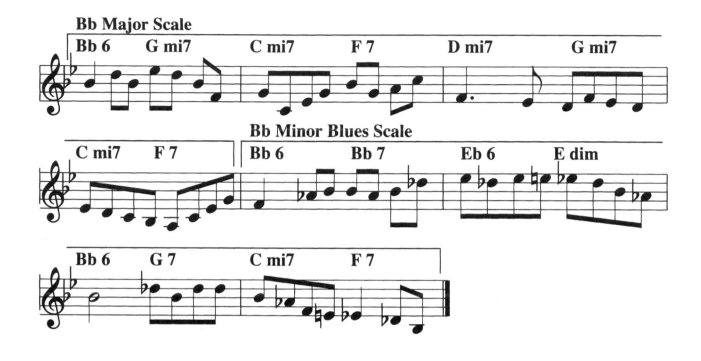

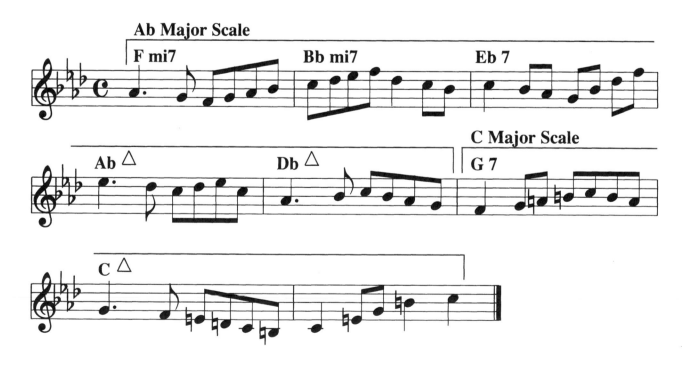

Pentatonic scales are useful in bracketing since they have five tones which can be superimposed in more than one place on certain types of chords. The same scale can be analyzed differently in relation to a series of chords and fit them all equally well. The next example is the same common progression used in the previous example but this time bracketed with two different pentatonic scales.

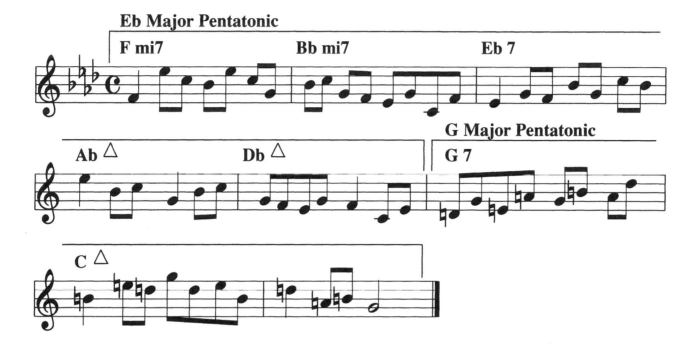

An adventuresome form of bracketing is utilized in some approaches to "outside" playing and often involves the use of pentatonics. Ramon Ricker's book on pentatonic scales is a good source for some of those techniques.

Summary:

1) Bracketing produces the strongest sense of the tonalities since it implies using the major or minor scales of key areas.

2) Bracketing keys is the simplest approach to chord/scale relationships since the fewest number of scales is used.

3) Using a simple approach doesn't mean it's bad, nor does a complex approach mean it's good.

4) Tunes that primarily involve chords of one key may be bracketed using the least number of scales.

Chapter 4 - Implications
of Chord Symbols ──────

Much contemporary music is very colorful and draws heavily on the use of either chromatic tones (approaches) or altered scales which include tones foreign to the key. As creative improvisors, we quickly find ways to enhance simple chord progressions and "spice" them up with the use of altered scales which introduce chromatic tension. However, it's important to distinguish between situations which allow for and really need chromatic alteration and those which should be treated with more purity and respect for the implications of the basic chord symbols.

For example, in a simple chord progression such as blues, there may be few indications of specific alterations in the chord symbols. The improvisor may then have a generally free hand in choosing the kinds of sounds he wants to use for variety and interest. Even when some alterations are specified, there's still a certain artistic license that may be exercised by enhancing the changes with more alterations. An important consideration to keep in mind is this: Does the addition of a particular alteration change the basic character of a chord?

For example, if a natural 5th is a prominent melody note and a very distinctive aspect of that part of the

---

Does the addition of a particular alteration change the basic character of a chord?

---

tune, introducing an altered 5th may change the character of the sound in a way that isn't desired. Remember, if the composer had wanted that sound in the piece, he probably would have shown it either in the chord symbol or in the actual melody itself. So, always begin by supplying only what's called for.

In the early '70s, it was very fashionable among some players to add the alteration of a raised 5th to major 7th chords. However, if you try imposing this alteration on <u>any</u> major 7th chord, you'll discover a drastic change in the character of the sound. The following example shows this type of alteration to the major 7th chords found in the first eight measures of a very common chord progression.

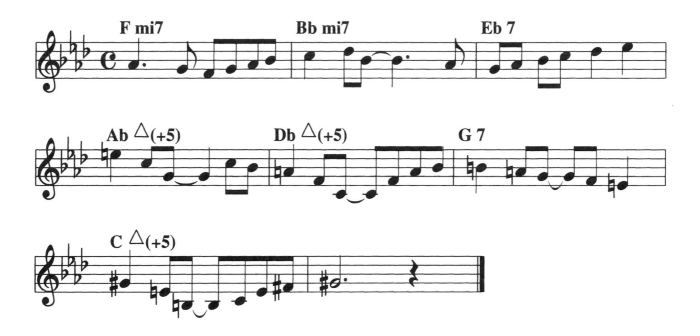

However, for dominant chords, if any alterations are present in the chord symbol, we don't mind and even prefer additional alterations. For example, if an altered 5th is specified, we usually don't object to the 9th being altered as well. Or if an altered 9th is called for, we could supply an altered 5th also. The only caution is to be careful of any implications of the melody.

In the following example, a dominant 7th with an altered 5th is functioning as a V chord of the key. Since there's no reference to the 9th, an additional altered 9th could be used and the next improvised line shows this. Dominant chords functioning as V often sound good with extra alterations. Generally, if either an altered 5th or altered 9th is called for, the other is added.

In the next example, however, the melody emphasizes a natural 5th so altering the 5th will change the character of the sound in a way that may not be desirable.

Since the '60s, composers have tended to be quite specific in their use of chord symbols. This seems to indicate that they hear distinct and subtle differences in the various chords in a piece. To add alterations in a situation such as this may be an irresponsible act by the improvisor. As was stated earlier in the book, if an improvisor doesn't like the sound of the chords as originally composed, he should write his own similar, yet different, composition. The original wishes of the composer must be recognized and respected. Therefore, the next consideration to keep in mind is this: Are the chord symbols very specific in their indications of subtle differences between chord sounds?

Generally, a guideline to follow might be this: If the piece contains chords of the same category with different alterations, treat them as specifically as possible. For example, if there's both a dom7+9 and a dom7+5+9, the two chords should be treated with two distinct sounds instead of using the same +5+9 sound on both. The composer must have heard a difference between the two and the improvisor must also make the distinction.

Are the chord symbols very specific in their indications of subtle differences between chord sounds?

Remember, a large variety of chord sounds may be one of the most interesting aspects of a piece. To blatantly "plug in" your own scale choices without regard for signals to you from the composer is like climbing onto a harmonic bulldozer and leveling out the different colors of the tune to a single sound.

The following example is a chord progression with a variety of chord sounds in major, minor and dominant families with the specific scales implied by each. This chord progression calls for good security with a variety of scales but has a lot of harmonic interest to it.

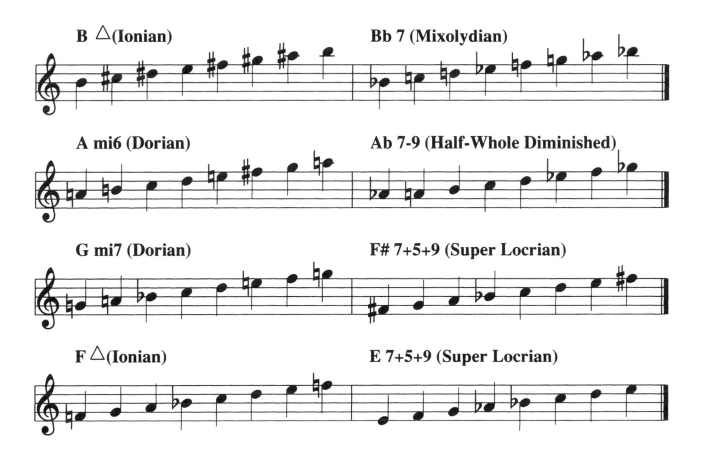

Summary:

1) With dominant chords, if any alterations are present in the chord symbol, it's usually acceptable to supply additional alterations.

2) Care must be taken that the addition of an alteration doesn't change the basic character of a chord sound.

3) If the piece contains chords of the same category with different alterations, treat them as specifically as possible.

Chapter 5 - Implications of the Melody

Some melodies are simply less interesting and really have little to do with the "sound" of a piece. Many "jam session" types of tunes have melodies that improvisors view as nothing more than a line to set up the soloists' individual statements. In fact, the main business at hand may simply be good sport involving the passing around of musical ideas among soloists much like a musical game of Frisbee.

However, a song with a really interesting chord progression and a well-written melody is truly a thing of beauty. If you stop to think of reasons that you find a particular tune attractive as a vehicle, you'll often realize that the melody is a big

---

What an improvisor often doesn't consider is the importance of the melody to the "aura" of the piece.

---

factor in your choice. What an improvisor often doesn't consider is the importance of the melody to the "aura" of the piece. If you recall that many tunes share very similar or identical chord progressions, then you begin to understand the true importance of the melody.

Consider a "blindfold test" in which you're listening to the radio, you've missed hearing the melody played, and you're trying to decide what the tune is by listening for the chord progression and also to the chord/scales being used by different soloists. It's often difficult to tell for certain, although your ability to hear chord progressions may be very good. One of the main reasons for this difficulty may be the soloist's failure to render the true sound of the piece. This is probably because the chord/scales that he has chosen don't accurately reflect the aura created by the melody.

When an improvisor really has the melody of a song in his head, you can "hear" it in his solo. Not only that, but often you can sing the melody with the improvisation and find that it fits. This shows a high level of improvisation which, ironically, is very basic to what I think an improvisor's goal should be: To try to create new melodies that retain the sound of the original melody.

In the days of traditional jazz, improvisation was often nothing more than "hot" melody playing, that is, using extra embellishments with the melody. Many players had little or no theoretical training and used only their ears and a sense of the key center to guide their solos. So, the melody was often a "security blanket" which helped them to keep their place and stay in the right sounds. It's unfortunate that we've lost some of that spirit in the art of improvisation since we can make very effective use of melodic fragments in our solos.

A classical work usually has a large section which is devoted to developing the important melodic themes. Isn't an improvised solo really just another form of development section? If the improvisation is to have anything to do with the composition, then it would seem that it should draw on at least some of the melodic material. The fringe benefit

Isn't an improvised solo really just another form of development section?

is an assurance that the solo will sound as if it fits the piece.

The melody has implications which sometimes are obvious and other times can be very subtle but are felt and heard nevertheless. If melodic motives aren't used, a solo should at least use the same scales.

The next examples show some melodies with chord symbols that don't imply only one chord/scale. But, if scale choices are made that reflect implications of the melody, some compositional integrity is achieved and the improvisation should sound the same as the piece on which it's based.

In the first example, the melody suggests an Ionian scale instead of a Lydian scale, because there's a natural 4th scale step present.

In the second example, Aeolian is suggested because of the lowered 6th scale step in the melody.

The next example contains distinctive alterations in positions of strong emphasis. The -9 and +5 in this melody would suggest that the dominant 7th chord be satisfied with either the Super Locrian scale or the 5th mode of the harmonic minor.

In the following example, the chord symbol includes the alteration of a raised 7th, but the melody also includes a raised 6th scale step which would then suggest ascending melodic minor rather than harmonic minor.

The last example shows a tune that arpeggiates the harmony but, since it utilizes only basic chord tones, it doesn't give any clues as to the final choice of a chord/scale. Practically any dominant 7th scale could be used for improvisation in this case.

There may still be other factors involved in the final chord/scale choice, but the melody is certainly one of the most important.

Summary:

1) What an improvisor often doesn't consider is the importance of the melody to the general "aura" of the piece.

2) An improvisor's goal should be to try to create new melodies that retain the sound of the original melody.

3) If an alteration or some scale degree which is peculiar to a certain mode is present in the melody, this should be reflected in the choice of a scale for improvisation.

Chapter 6 - Implications of Function

A good understanding of chord function can help you make sensible decisions about which chord/scales to use. There's a natural relationship of the modes of major or minor scales to the function of chords in the keys. For example, if a chord is a tonic (I) function built on a major

---

There's a natural relationship of the modes of major or minor scales to the function of chords in the keys.

---

key center, it makes sense that the major scale built on the same note will produce the sound of that key. Also, if a chord is a II chord built on the 2nd scale step of that same major key, then the Dorian mode built on its root will again produce the same tones of that major key. This same rationale can be applied to chords built on other scale degrees as well.

In similar fashion, modes of the harmonic minor tend to line up with functions in a minor key. The harmonic minor is generally the choice to generate modes in most minor keys, because it supplies the leading tone (raised 7th) that we're traditionally accustomed to hearing. However, when the leading tone isn't wanted or needed, a mode of the pure minor (or relative major) may be used.

On the next page is a chart that summarizes all the functions, chord types and the chord/scales which accompany them for both major and minor keys. When used in these common relationships, these modes will sustain and reinforce the sound of the key area. Notice in the Minor Key summary, that the scales listed are either consistent with the pure minor tonality or imply the use of the leading tone (raised 7th).

Major Key

Function	Chord Type	Chord/Scale
I	Major 7th	Ionian (major)
II	Minor 7th	Dorian
III	Minor 7th	Phrygian
IV	Major 7th	Lydian
V	Dominant 7th	Mixolydian
VI	Minor 7th	Aeolian (pure minor)
VII	Half-Diminished	Locrian

Minor Key

Function	Chord Type	Chord/Scale
I	Minor 7th	H.M. or Aeolian
II	Half-Diminished	2nd mode H.M. or Locrian
III	Major 7th	Ionian
IV	Minor 7th	4th mode H.M. or Dorian
V	Dominant 7th	5th mode H.M.
VI	Major 7th	6th mode H.M. or Lydian
#VI	Half-Diminished	6th mode M.M. or Locrian
VII	Dominant 7th	Mixolydian
#VII	Diminished	7th mode of H.M.

H.M. = Harmonic Minor; M.M. = Ascending Melodic Minor

Observing the previous choices for functional harmony isn't the only approach available to an improvisor. However, this will ensure that the tonality isn't confused or obscured by the introduction of tones which normally aren't present. A desired musical effect may call for a choice which introduces an unexpected sound. But, most of the time the best result will come from the use of the normal choice.

Since the modes of major or harmonic minor scales line up so well with functions, you can use this natural persuasion as a way to create an interesting musical effect. For example, we expect to hear the 5th mode of harmonic minor used with a dominant (V) chord in minor. If we use that mode with the V chord in major, we'll create the suggestion of a resolution to a minor tonic (I) chord. The major I chord will seem like a fresh surprise when normally it would have sounded very natural.

The use of an inappropriate mode can create an awkward effect. For instance, if a Mixolydian mode is used with a V chord in minor, it suggests a major key and the resolution to minor can sound very strange.

Any dominant 7th chord which resolves up a 4th or down a 5th tends to assume a V function even if it's a V of some other chord of the key. If the resolution of a dominant 7th is to a major chord, almost any dominant 7th scale may be used with the exception of blues. If the resolution is to a minor chord, the 5th mode of harmonic minor or a Super Locrian scale should be used to reinforce the minor tonality. The next example shows a progression with an A7 (VI7) chord moving up a perfect 4th to a D minor chord, the II chord in C major.

In the previous example, it's important to realize that although the progression is in the key of C, A7 to Dmi7 is a V to I relationship. So, by using D harmonic minor with the A7 chord, the resolution to the Dmi7 will seem natural.

Tri-tone substitutions which resolve down a half step (such as Db7 to Cmi7) must be treated very carefully. However, here are several formulas regarding the substitution of sounds a tri-tone apart that will be helpful to remember:

1. A Super Locrian scale and a Lydian, b7 scale located a tri-tone apart have the same tones (ie. G Super Locrian = Db Lydian, b7.)

2. Two Half-Whole Diminished scales located a tri-tone apart have the same tones (ie. G Half-Whole Diminished = Db Half-Whole Diminished.)

3. Two Whole Tone scales located a tri-tone apart have the same tones (ie. G Whole Tone = Db Whole Tone.)

As mentioned before, with a V chord resolving up a 4th to a minor chord, one of the best choices is a Super Locrian scale. If there has been a tri-tone substitution which results in a resolution down a half step, then a Lydian, b7 scale should be used. This supplies the same tones as the Super Locrian scale would have on the original V chord.

Notice that the following two scales contain the same tones:

G Super Locrian - G Ab Bb Cb Db Eb F G
Db Lydian, b7   - Db Eb F G Ab Bb Cb Db

Summary:

1) There's a natural relationship of the modes of major or minor scales to the function of chords in the respective keys.

2) The choice of the appropriate scale in relation to a particular function will reinforce the tonality.

3) The choice of an optional scale can create the suggestion of a different function or another key.

Chapter 7 - Implications of Context

No chord is an island isolated from other chords. We normally deal with chord progressions, that is, series of chords which relate to each other in a horizontal time continuum. Therefore, each chord, though it may call for a specific sound, must be considered in the context of the entire progression. It's important to understand the functional relationships of chords to major or minor keys; it's even more important that we understand the relationship of two successive chords to each other.

As players (and listeners) we're all affected by our tonal memory, that is, our ability to remember what we've just heard for even a few seconds. Your subconscious mind has the marvelous ability to record notes going by in an instant and to provide you with a reference point for future musical events. Based on the memory of what happened in the recent musical past (a beat or two before), you perceive various sounds as meeting expectations or as surprises, both pleasant and tense. Generally, if your expectation is met, the result is relaxing; if a surprise occurs, the result is tense or exciting. Tension and relaxation are both important relative qualities in music and should generally be present in some balance.

The context in which a chord occurs may be the final part of being able to make a chord/scale choice. Alterations or extensions may not be specified in the chord symbol, the melody may lack any implications and the function may be either unclear or twofold (a dual function). Therefore, what tones are sounding on either side of the chord being considered can provide important clues to chord/scale choice.

Generally, changing as few notes as possible, or letting as much of what we've been hearing continue into the next chord, is accepted by our ears as sounding good. When tones are changed that don't have to change, the result may be a fresh sound that's attractive, or it could be something that sounds forced and unnatural. Probably a good rule to follow would be: If in doubt whether or not to change a note that doesn't have to change, don't.

If in doubt whether or not to change a note that doesn't have to change, don't.

The first example shows how the context in which a chord is found may help the determination of a chord/scale. The chord symbol calls for a +11 and the C7 is a V function. There's not really enough information to make the final choice of a chord/scale since there's more than one dominant 7th scale that includes a +11. Therefore, the chord has to be examined in the context of both the preceding and following chords. In this case, both of those chord/scales include a G natural and a D natural. These tones would be reflected in the C7 as a natural 5th and 9th. That would tend to rule out any dominant 7th scales which include altered 5ths or 9ths. Therefore, the "best" choice in this context (the scale that creates the smoothest flow) would be a Lydian, b7 scale. This choice satisfies the +11 which is specified, has a natural 5th and 9th, and only one tone has to change (B to Bb) from the G major scale that comes before it.

It should be pointed out that almost any dominant 7th scale could be used on the C7 in the preceding example since it functions as a V chord in major and the symbol has no specific requirements. And, this would be true of any dominant 7th chord that resolves down a 5th or up a 4th. The point here is that, in this context, the C7 will have a smoother flow when satisfied with the Lydian, b7 scale.

Sometimes, music contains non-functional harmony, the chord symbols are general and the melody doesn't imply any alterations. The context in which a chord occurs may be the only factor which will help resolve the final decision of a chord/scale. The following example shows a progression which contains non-functional harmony and has no helpful information supplied in the chord symbols.

In the preceding example, only two notes have to change in going from the C Maj7 to Bb7, Bb and Ab, the root and 7th of the Bb7. All the other tones of the C major scale can be carried over. This implies the use of a Lydian, b7 scale on the Bb7, which would create the smoothest flow from one chord to the next and create a relaxing effect.

However, prepared with this information, you could then elect to use other options such as a diminished scale on the Bb7. This would introduce a C# that wasn't heard in the C major scale and add an element of tension.

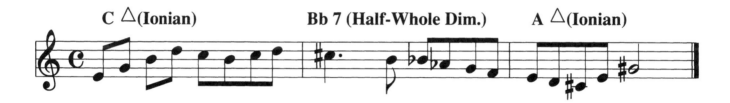

Even in functional situations that are normal, you can use the awareness of context and tonal memory to create just the effect you want. In the following progression, the two chords can be bracketed with the same scale since the root progression is I to VII in a major key. The expectation is Locrian on the D half-diminished chord.

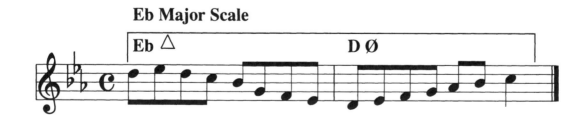

However, if you wanted to inject an element of surprise, you could elect to use a Locrian, #2 scale with the D Ø. The E natural supplied by that scale wouldn't be present in one's tonal memory and would sound quite fresh.

The point is that both choices in the previous examples satisfy the D Ø chord adequately. The first one fulfills an expectation based on your recent experience (tonal memory) and the second creates a surprise which is unexpected. The first of these examples is relaxed in nature but the second produces an element of tension.

Sometimes, you can make the transition between two chords very smooth or you can exaggerate the difference. In the next progression, the chords have no relationship; so it's a matter of deciding what tones must change and which ones can stay the same. In this case, E Aeolian to G Dorian (one # to one b) creates the smoothest change.

If you wanted to make the key change from E minor to G minor seem more dramatic, choices could be made which involved more tones changing from one chord to the next.

In the following example, E Dorian to G Aeolian (two #'s to two b's) results in an extreme change since more tones are different in the G scale than stay the same.

There are two other possible options which could have been used above. They would result in more change than the first example but less than the second. If the choice was E Dorian to G Dorian, it would result in a change of three notes (two #'s to one b). If the choice was E Aeolian to G Aeolian, it would also result in a change of three tones (one # to two b's). Both combinations would be equally smooth but the Dorian version would probably seem brighter.

When examining the context in which a chord occurs, more weight is usually placed on the effect of a previous chord since we carry the tonal memory of it. However, you may prefer to anticipate the following chord by making a choice which flows naturally and smoothly into it, even though the current sound is a brief surprise. Also, if the chord in question is functioning in more than one way at the same time, you may choose to stress its relationship to one key more than the other.

The next example shows the common occurrence of a C minor chord that functions as I in C minor and II in Bb major. If the G7 and Cmi7 chords are bracketed with a C harmonic minor scale, the Cmi7 will seem more like a I chord and the F7 will be more of a surprise.

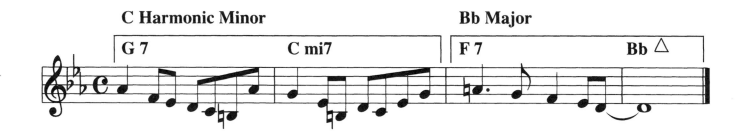

However, if Dorian is used on the Cmi7, it'll create more of a surprise at that point. The flow into the F7 will sound very smooth and meet a normal expectation. Either way, you can control where the surprise takes place.

The next example shows a dominant 7th functioning as both V in Bb major and as a bII tri-tone substitution for the V in E minor. If Mixolydian is used, then the F7 will sound natural following Bb major, but the B natural that occurs in the E minor chord will be surprising.

If a Lydian, b7 scale is used, the F7 will sound surprising but will flow very naturally into the E minor.

Summary:

1) Generally, if your expectation is met, the result is relaxing; if a surprise occurs, the result is tense or exciting.

2) If in doubt whether or not to change a note that doesn't have to change, don't.

3) Some questions to use as guidelines:

   a) What sound creates the smoothest flow from the previous chord to the present one?

   b) Do you want to meet the normal expectation based on tonal memory or create a surprise?

   c) In a dual function situation, do you want to sustain a current tonality or anticipate a new one?

Chapter 8 - A Perspective on Roots

We're taught to build chords from the root, chord symbols always include the root of a chord, and we're generally aware of the root progressions (the distance between roots of chords). However, too much preoccupation with roots of chords can be a serious limitation to a developing improvisor.

It's obvious when an improvisor doesn't know a certain chord/scale and clings to the root of the chord as a security blanket. Naturally, it's important to know the traditions of our music and to be comfortable with all facets of root progressions in harmony. But, at some point, the root becomes a crutch that must be cast aside if an improvisor ever wants to "run" with confidence. Also, a root can actually be heard without anyone playing it.

Ultimately, the important thing is understanding what the total sound is at any given point, ie. what's the complete set of notes in effect? We've already seen that the same set of notes can be described as either a chord or a scale. We've also learned that the same scale can be described as several different scales. Therefore, why not take the same view of chords and become more familiar with all the chords within a chord and not be overly concerned with what the root is?

For example, within a single 13th chord, there are five different 7th chords and six different triads. The following example shows the triads and 7th chords which are found within a C mi13 chord:

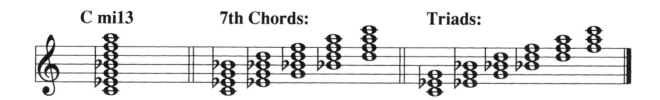

In spite of the root, these chords are present within the sound and are heard, at least to some extent. The implication of this to the improvisor is that there may be functional relationships present in a chord progression that don't appear to exist.

In the following example, there's a V to I relationship present, though the root progression is V to IV. The I chord is present as the 5th, 7th, 9th and +11th of the IV chord.

$$\text{Eb } \triangle 7+11 = \text{Eb G} \boxed{\text{Bb D F A}}$$

$$\text{Bb } \triangle 7 \quad\quad = \quad\quad \boxed{\text{Bb D F A}}$$

Sometimes scale or chord tones other than the roots can be considered roots to allow you to view a progression from another perspective. For instance, in the following progression, Bb7 is a part of the D half-diminished sound and Eb is part of the C minor sound. So the progression could be viewed as Bb7 to Eb Maj7, or a V to I function. The chord/scales would be exactly the same; D Locrian = Bb Mixolydian and C Aeolian = Eb Major. Also, the chords are common tone substitutions for each other. However, the main point here is that this presents a different way of looking at this chord progression.

Surprisingly, ideas that would be used over a V to I progression will often sound good and be just as effective, even if the roots aren't V to I. This can be a device to open your conception and expand your active vocabulary, often vocabulary you already possess.

Another reason to attribute less importance to roots is that it may interfere with your awareness of guide tones or leading tones in the harmony. Often root movements are by intervals of a 4th up or 5th down, very jagged melodic intervals. If you've ever heard an improvisor play a cycling progression and give too much stress to the roots of the chords, you know what poor kinds of melodies result. If you study the polyphonic writing of the Baroque period, which was often based on cycling progressions, you see the true mastery of melodic voice-leading and compound melodies built on key guide tones.

Consider the next progression and recall from earlier examples, that it can be bracketed with only two scales. So, in a sense, there are only two keys or "roots" present. Notice the guide tones which are the 3rds and 7ths of each chord.

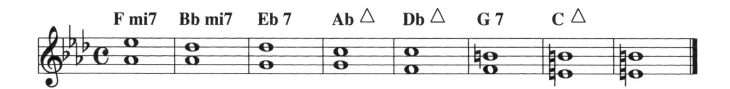

In the previous example, the root movements of a 5th are less important than the resolutions of 7ths to 3rds which act as guide tones moving through the progression. A skillful improvisor will use these guide tones as anchor points for his melodic ideas as follows.

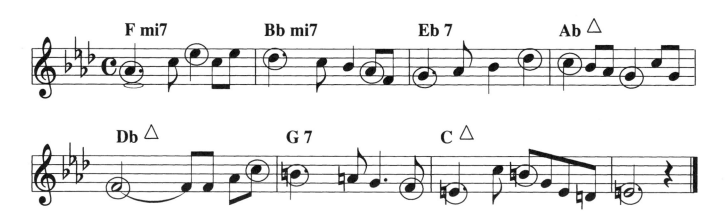

Sometimes, as in a major 7th chord, the root isn't a good note to stress unless it's played in a low register by an instrument such as trombone, baritone sax or bass. If it's played in a middle register, the typical location of most piano and guitar chord voicings, there's a good chance it'll clash with the major 7th, which is the characteristic tone of the chord anyway. So, other than passing over the root while moving through a scale at medium to fast speed, it's a good idea to avoid stressing it in a melodic idea. A good way to do this is to "change" the root of a major 7th in your mind. For example, you can think of the 3rd or 5th of the chord as the root. Neither of the chords built on those notes include the original root, so you might be less inclined to stress it. In the next example, a G Maj7 is outlined instead of a C Maj7 and the root is automatically avoided. This also creates a Lydian sound since the raised 4th of the C scale is stressed.

Another advantage to changing the root in your mind is that you can create more of a polychordal sound. For example, if you assign the 9th as the root, you'll stress a triad which emphasizes the 9th. +11th and 13th of the chord. This will produce the illusion of playing in another key when you are simply giving more emphasis to the upper extensions of the chord. The following melody is an example of this.

In non-functional harmony, there may be no key relationships apparent and yet there may still be normal functions if you assign other tones the roles of becoming the roots. In the following progression, Eb Ma7+5 to A mi9, there appears to be no relationship between the two chords. However, if you assign a specific mode to each chord, then other root possibilities appear. For instance, the Lydian-Augmented scale that goes with the Eb Maj+5 is the same set of tones as a B Super Locrian scale. The Dorian scale that might be used with the A mi9 is the same set of tones as those found in an E Aeolian scale.

Eb Lydian-Augmented = Eb F G A B C D Eb
B Super Locrian   = B C D Eb F G A B

A Dorian = A B C D E F# G A
E Aeolian = E F# G A B C D E

So, in actual sound, this progression could be considered to be B7+5+9 to E mi7 (V to I). In fact, the same language you might use over a B7+5+9 to E mi7 will sound very good as shown by the following example.

Summary:

1) The important thing is understanding what the total sound is at any given point.

2) A skillful improvisor will use guide tones as anchor points for his melodic ideas.

3) It's a good idea to avoid stressing the root in a melodic idea.

4) The roots of the chords aren't as important as the relationships of individual sets of tones (chord/scales) to each other.

Chapter 9 - Common Denominators and Color Progression —

In many challenging contemporary compositions confronting jazz improvisors, it isn't possible to use an understanding of function or to bracket keys with single scales. Usually, it's because the piece is in a constant state of modulation. Each chord in a series may call for a new sound with at least one or more tones that have to change from the previous chord/scale. Therefore, different tactics must be used.

One of the main points stressed in the last chapter was a de-emphasis of the importance of chord roots and the replacement of roots by other tones (substitute roots). This chapter will take those ideas a step further and suggest that the best approach may be to view a piece as having a color progression instead of a root progression. In some ways, this is like bracketing

keys except, in this case, you may only be able to come up with one tone in common with several chords instead of an entire scale.

Again, let's look at the common cycling progression which we have seen can be nicely bracketed with only two different scales. If we take this idea one step further, the whole eight bars can easily be bracketed with a single note G as the common denominator. Notice in the next example that even if the progression is bracketed with only two scales, there's an advantage to viewing those two scales based on a common denominator. In other words, you can view both sounds as being built on the same root. Now, there's no longer a progression of roots, but a color progression of five bars of a G Locrian scale to three bars of a G Mixolydian scale.

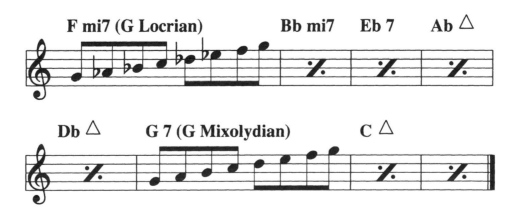

In the next example, a different chord/scale is assigned to each chord and there's always one or more tones that have to change from one chord to the next.

Now if the common denominator G is applied again, every scale can be viewed and understood as a G scale of some sort. In essence, the chords have become a color progression of G sounds.

Viewing the progression from this perspective increases awareness of the melodic guide tones, since all chord/scales are built on a common denominator, the note G.

There's an advantage to using this type of thinking on any tune. The more freedom a player has from dependency on the roots, the more melodic his improvisation may become. To put that another way, the more security an improvisor has with any given sound, the less need there is to give any concern to the chord roots.

We all learn modes from some parent scale, for instance, the seven modes of the major scale. But, why not learn the modes of any of those scales? For instance, Dorian has seven modes, Lydian has seven modes, etc. There can be a useful advantage to seeing any chord from another perspective. Try thinking of a minor chord sound as a Lydian scale on the 3rd instead of Dorian on the root. Consider a major chord as Ionian on the 5th instead of as Lydian on the root.

Try viewing the scale for a chord as starting on any note except the root. This is bound to enhance your security with the chord/scale since you have to be able to think of the sound in more than one way. The

Try viewing the scale for a chord as starting on any note except the root.

more different ways you can view a set of tones, the less you'll have to think about them.

In chord progressions, our ears will always be aware of the roots which are usually present and given considerable stress in the rhythm section. Moreover, we know the musical effect of stressing different chord tones in relation to the root, and we form preferences about those we like to hear.

Using common denominators and viewing a series of chords as a color progression doesn't conflict with the traditions of our music in any way. It's simply an expansion of the ways we can come closer to an understanding of the sounds we want. This is merely a methodical approach to analysis of chord/scales which can greatly simplify the task.

Summary:

1) The best approach may be to view a piece as having a color progression instead of a root progression.

2) The more freedom a player has from dependency on the roots, the more melodic his improvisation may become.

3) Building all of the scales on the same note increases awareness of the melodic guide tones.

Chapter 10 - Musical Traditions and Scale Choice

Most of us involved with music that is improvised are affected by two different musical traditions, the European-Classical tradition and the Jazz tradition. Because of our upbringing, our musical training and all of our experiences in music, we can't help being affected by these traditions. They are both valid and have an important connection to the art of improvisation.

As children, we participate in school bands, orchestras and choral groups, sing in church choirs, learn camp songs and study the classical literature on our instruments. We permanently store the memory of these sounds, which are based on the European-Classical tradition, in our subconscious minds. Stored

there, they influence our thinking (and hearing) for the rest of our lives. When we first learn about jazz harmony and the sounds unique to it, there may be some things which seem strange; but we become comfortable with that tradition as well.

Both of these traditions imply certain kinds of scales in relation to each family of chords. Since the classical tradition is based on major and minor keys, a major scale (or Ionian) is the normal expected sound with a major chord, and a pure minor scale (or Aeolian) is the expected sound with a minor chord. However, with the extended jazz harmonies such as major and minor 13th chords, we hear Lydian and Dorian scales implied.

The following chart summarizes the normal scale choices for each of the families of chords based on these traditions:

Chord Family	Classical Tradition	Jazz Tradition
Major 7th	Ionian (nat. 4)	Lydian (# 4)
Minor 7th	Aeolian (nat. 6)	Dorian (# 6)
Dominant 7th	Mixolydian (nat. 4)	Lydian, b7 (# 4)
Half-Diminished	Locrian (nat. 2)	Locrian, #2 (# 2)
Diminished	7th mode of H. M.	Whole-Half Diminished

The tones in parentheses distinguish the two choices for the same chord family.

These scale choices are broad generalizations. Things such as the chord symbols, the melody and function or context always have to come into consideration and may change any of these choices. Still, your choice of a chord/scale may turn out to be one of the above. In fact, you can often approach four of the families and their common choices with a question about which of two scale degrees is desired. For example, with a major 7th chord, do you want a natural 4th or a raised 4th; with a minor 7th chord, do you want a natural 6th or a raised 6th?

Many improvisors, when they discover attractive sounds such as Lydian and Dorian scales, become infatuated with these choices and tend to exclude more traditional sounds, such as Ionian and Aeolian from their vocabularies. This is really unfortunate for these reasons:

1. Every scale has its own unique, attractive beauty and has a certain inherent melodic potential.

2. No scale implies a specific style nor is it limited to exclusive use in only one tradition of music.

Another factor that influences some improvisors is the tendency to view some scales as being better or having a built-in key to melodic and musical success. Unfortunately, the use of the most complex or unique scale sound won't guarantee the success of a melody. A bad melody, even with the use of an unusual scale sound, is still a bad melody. It's essential that as an improvisor you develop a melodic sense using the simplest of materials, such as major and pure minor scales.

A bad melody, even with the use of an unusual scale sound, is still a bad melody.

The study of melody by itself would provide the basis for a whole book. It would probably call for some of the following activities:

1. The study of good melodies from all styles of music — classical, popular music, jazz, folk — and any other idioms that interest you.

2. The study of transcriptions of improvised solos.

3. The study of sight-singing and ear-training to develop a secure ability to sing a good melody without thinking of its theoretical structure.

4. The development of lyricism by emulating great musicians and imitating their vocabulary.

Summary:

Chord/scale choice can often be reduced to a set of simple questions for four chord families:

1) Major chords — Do you expect to hear a natural 4th or a raised 4th?

2) Minor chords — Do you expect to hear a natural 6th or a raised 6th?

3) Dominant 7ths — Do you expect to hear a natural 4th or a raised 4th?

4) Half-Diminished — Do you expect to hear a natural 2nd or a raised 2nd?

Chapter 11 - Scale Superimpositions ────────

As stated in the introduction, the main thrust of this book is to help musicians develop a way of thinking about the music they play. Then they can choose just the right sounds for the chords in progressions they wish to use as vehicles for improvisation. It's essential that you develop a command of the usual group of chord/scale choices and be able to discriminate between subtleties of nuance in chord sounds. However, a complete study of jazz chord/scales must include some consideration of the superimposition of scales that don't exactly fit the chords.

We start improvising mostly with our ears and instincts which often suggest the use of non-scale or non-chord tones. As we learn theory, we eliminate some of these "illegal" notes and find the sounds that exactly fit each chord. But as we evolve, we realize that melodic tension and interest may often call for the use of notes that aren't part of the pure sound of the harmony. Early jazz improvisors showed this with the use of "blue" notes such as the lowered 3rd and 7th over major chords. These non-chord tones produced a "bluesy" quality that has remained an essential element of our music today. It's still very important to be able to play "right" notes (scales that exactly fit each of the harmonies). However, it's also essential to know how to use "wrong" notes (scales that don't fit the harmonies exactly).

The following example illustrates the use of a "wrong note" scale for the improvisation:

The following chart shows some scales which are commonly superimposed on the wrong chord types for a certain musical effect. Included in the chart are the chord family, the scale superimposition and its normal use. The "wrong" notes are in parentheses:

Chord Family	Scale Superimposition	Normal Use
Major	Mixolydian (b7)	Dominant 7th
Major	Dorian (b3, b7)	Minor 7th
Major	W 1/2 Dim. (b3, b5, #5)	Diminished 7th
Major	Minor Blues (b3, b5, b7)	Minor 7th
Dominant	Dorian (b3)	Minor 7th
Dominant	Minor Blues (b3, b5)	Minor 7th
Minor	W 1/2 Dim. (b5, #5, Δ7)	Diminished 7th

Notice in the previous chart that many superimpositions add lowered 3rds or 7ths and create a bluesy feel. Again, good melodic sense will guide you in the choice of these sounds which may not even be superimpositions but instead a skillful use of the non-chord/scale tones, which are commonly called

---

If handled carefully, any of the twelve chromatic pitches may be used in relation to any type of chord.

---

approaches. If handled carefully, any of the twelve chromatic pitches may be used in relation to any type of chord. Some notes are consonant (chord tones), some are moderately consonant (scale tones) and some are dissonant (non-scale tones). Bebop musicians of the '50s made every attempt to utilize dissonant non-scale tones to create surprising musical effects. Accordingly, it was a basic foundation of bebop to be able to use approach tones skillfully. However, the chromatic "wrong" notes usually resolve by half-step to adjacent chord tones to relax the harmonic tension.

Establishing priorities in your growth as an improvisor is important. The following list might be a good order for some of these priorities:

1) First learn to play "right" notes; that is, the correct chord/scale tones that exactly fit chords.

2) Next learn to use approaches, the non-scale tones that exist in addition to the scale tones.

3) Lastly, experiment with the superimposition of the "wrong" scale sounds over chords.

Remember there are usually between 5 and 8 scale tones that fit a chord sound. The applicability of the remaining 4 to 7 non-scale tones will depend on the kind of musical effect wanted. Generally, more chromatic tension will be a normal result and, since our music is very chromatic in nature, this may be just the desired effect.

Summary:

1) Melodic tension and interest may often call for the use of notes that aren't part of the pure sound of the harmony.

2) If handled carefully, any of the twelve chromatic pitches may be used in relation to any chord.

Chapter 12 - Pentatonic Scales ———

A pentatonic scale is unique for several reasons: 1) It only contains five different tones, so it seems like something between an arpeggio and a scale; 2) Normally, a pentatonic scale includes only consonant intervals such as major 2nds, major or minor 3rds, and perfect 4ths; 3) All modes of a pentatonic scale are not used; 4) Usually one or more forms of the scale may be superimposed in several places on different types of chords; and 5) When it is superimposed properly on various chords, the scale has no "wrong" or dissonant sounding notes.

The pentatonic scale has had an interesting role in jazz. It first appeared as a natural outgrowth of the arpeggiation of 6th chords in earlier music. Many swing era cliches that most musicians can quote are usually pentatonic in their structure. Teachers who advocate the use of pentatonic scales to teach beginning improvisation can argue convincingly that they help develop a sense of the jazz tradition.

In contemporary music, there's such a variety of modal scale sounds available that pentatonic scales aren't needed and many players don't use them. However, since the early '60s, an increasing number of players have found the pentatonic scale very versatile in its ability to stress different aspects of the same chord sound by superimposing it on the chord in various locations. Also, the scale has proven to be a good resource for generating "fourthy" melodic shapes as opposed to many bebop cliches which were generally ideas arpeggiated in thirds.

The first example shows the major pentatonic and its "relative minor," the minor pentatonic. Notice that they both contain the same pitches starting on different tones.

Though it isn't necessary to use all five modes, there may be some value in using these two since they relate to major and minor tonalities. Some players use only the major form of the scale; but, when it's used with a minor chord, it may seem "minorish" in its sound. Also, there are some useful chord/scale relationships that are consistent with both the major and minor forms of the scale.

The next example shows a major pentatonic superimposed on the root, 5th and 9th of a major chord and a minor pentatonic superimposed on the root, 5th and 9th of a minor chord.

Note in the previous example that, when the pentatonic scale is superimposed on a higher chord tone, more of the upper extensions of the harmonies are emphasized. The main potential of pentatonic scales is that certain aspects of a chord sound may be emphasized and certain tones avoided. Since the scale only contains five tones, it's very flexible in its ability to fit into several locations on the same chord family and yet have different harmonic implications.

Notice the variety of dominant 7th chord sounds that can be achieved by various superimpositions as shown in the following example:

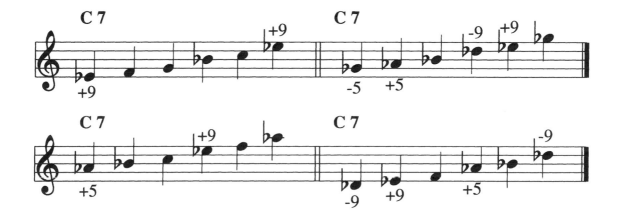

Finally, some mention should be made of the synthetic pentatonic scales needed to fit many kinds of chords. Neither the major nor the minor form of the scale fits a minor 6th chord. But by either lowering the 3rd tone of a major pentatonic or lowering the 5th tone of a minor pentatonic, the minor 6th chord sound can be easily reinforced.

There are many chords that require a synthetic pentatonic to satisfy the sound. As long as the scale structure is a combination of 2nds and 3rds which evenly divide the octave, the effect will be pentatonic in character.

Summary:

1) Many swing era cliches that most musicians can quote are usually pentatonic in their structure.

2) The pentatonic scale may be superimposed on the same chord in various locations to stress different aspects of the sound.

3) The pentatonic scale has proven to be a good resource for generating "fourthy" melodic shapes.

4) A synthetic pentatonic may be easily formed to fit any chord by simply choosing the major or minor form closest to the sound and then raising or lowering a tone.

Appendix I
Analysis of Compositions

Aspiration

Dan Haerle

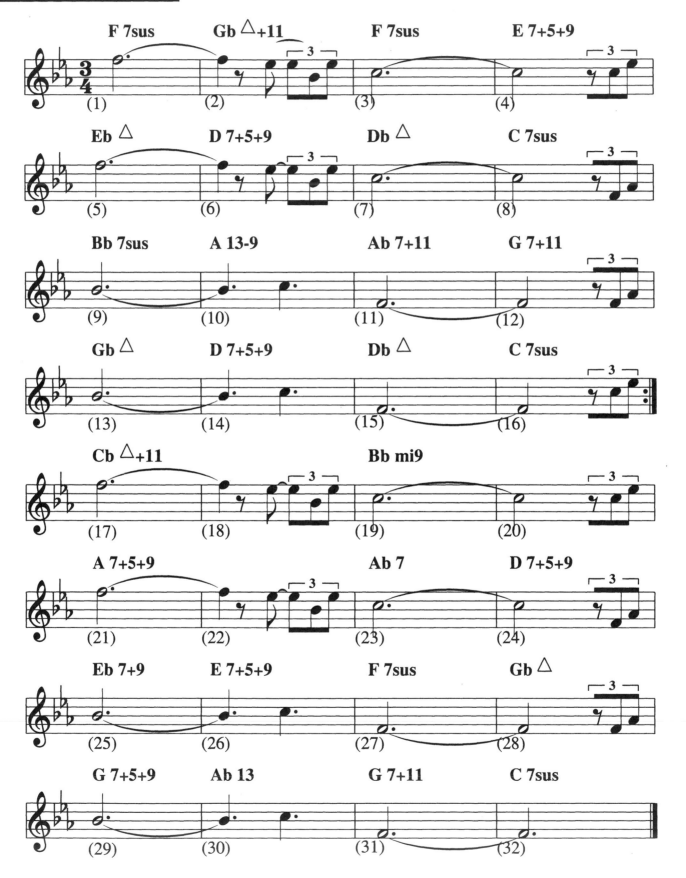

Aspiration - Analysis:

Bar	Chord	Chord/Scale	Considerations
1	F 7sus	Mixolydian	Dominant 7th with sus4
2	Gb Δ+11	Lydian	+4 in previous chord/scale
3	F 7sus	Mixolydian	Dominant 7th with sus4
4	E 7+5+9	Super Locrian	Altered 5th and 9th required
5	Eb Δ	Ionian	Natural 4 in previous chord/scale
6	D 7+5+9	Super Locrian	Altered 5th and 9th required
7	Db Δ	Ionian	Natural 4 in previous chord/scale
8	C 7sus	Mixolydian	Dominant 7th with sus4
9	Bb 7sus	Mixolydian	Dominant 7th with sus4
10	A 13-9	Half-Whole Dim.	Natural 13 and -9 required
11	Ab 7+11	Half-Whole Dim.	Chromatic sequence of sounds
12	G 7+11	Half-Whole Dim.	Chromatic sequence of sounds
13	Gb Δ	Ionian	Natural 4 in previous chord/scale
14	D 7+5+9	Super Locrian	Altered 5th and 9th required
15	Db Δ	Ionian	Natural 4 in previous chord/scale
16	C 7sus	Mixolydian	Dominant 7th with sus4
17	Cb Δ+11	Lydian	+4 in previous chord/scale
19	Bb mi9	Aeolian	Natural 6 in previous chord/scale
21	A 7+5+9	Super Locrian	Altered 5th and 9th required
23	Ab 7	Mixolydian	Natural 4 in previous chord/scale
24	D 7+5+9	Super Locrian	Altered 5th and 9th required
25	Eb 7+9	Half-Whole Dim.	+9 required
26	E 7+5+9	Super Locrian	Altered 5th and 9th required
27	F 7sus	Mixolydian	Dominant 7th with sus4
28	Gb Δ	Lydian	+4 in previous chord/scale
29	G 7+5+9	Super Locrian	Altered 5th and 9th required
30	Ab 13	Mixolydian	Natural 4 in previous chord/scale
31	G 7+11	Super Locrian	Altered 5 and 9 in previous sound
32	C 7sus	Mixolydian	Dominant 7th with sus4

Darin Rae

Dan Haerle

Darin Rae - Analysis:

Bar	Chord	Chord/Scale	Considerations
1	G △	Ionian	Natural 4 in previous chord/scale
2	F △+11	Lydian	+4 in previous chord/scale
3	E △	Ionian	Natural 4 in previous chord/scale
4	D △+11	Lydian	+4 in previous chord/scale
5	C# mi9	Aeolian	Natural 6 in previous chord/scale
6	C △	Lydian	+4 in previous chord/scale
7	B mi9	Aeolian	Natural 6 in previous chord/scale
9	Ab 7sus	Mixolydian	Dominant 7th with sus 4
10	Ab 13-9	Half-Whole Dim.	Natural 13 and -9 required
11	E △	Ionian	Natural 4 in previous chord/scale
12	F 7+5+9	Super Locrian	Altered 5th and 9th required
12	F 13-9	Half-Whole Dim.	Natural 13 and -9 required
13	Bb △	Ionian	Natural 4 in previous chord/scale
14	G 7sus	Mixolydian	Dominant 7th with sus 4
14	G 13-9	Half-Whole Dim.	Natural 13 and -9 required
15	C △	Ionian	Natural 4 in previous chord/scale
16	C# Ø	Locrian	II function
16	F# 7+5	Whole Tone	Dominant 7th with +5
17	B △	Ionian	Natural 4 in previous chord/scale
18	A# Ø	Locrian	VII function, same as previous sound
19	A △	Lydian	+4 in previous chord/scale
20	G △+11	Lydian	+4 in previous chord/scale
21	F# mi9	Aeolian	Natural 6 in previous chord/scale
22	F △+11	Lydian	+4 in previous chord/scale
23	Eb △	Ionian	I function
24	Ab △+11	Lydian	+4 in previous chord/scale

Driftin'

Dan Haerle

Driftin' - Analysis:

Bar	Chord	Chord/Scale	Considerations
1	A Δ	Ionian	I function, nat. 4 in previous sound
2	D Δ	Lydian	IV function, +4 in previous sound
3	A Δ	Ionian	I function, nat. 4 in previous sound
4	D Δ	Lydian	IV function, +4 in previous sound
5	A Δ	Ionian	I function, nat. 4 in previous sound
5	Ab Δ	Ionian or Lydian	Personal taste
6	G Δ	Ionian or Lydian	Personal taste
6	F Δ	Lydian	+4 in previous sound
7	Bb Δ	Lydian	IV function, +4 in previous sound
8	B 13+11	Lydian, b7	+11 required
9	E Δ	Ionian	I function, nat. 4 in previous sound
10	Eb 7+9	Half-Whole Dim.	+9 required
11	Ab Δ	Ionian	I function, nat. 4 in previous sound
12	Eb 7sus	Mixolydian	Dominant 7th with sus 4
13	Ab Δ	Ionian	I function, nat. 4 in previous sound
14	Eb 7sus	Mixolydian	Dominant 7th with sus 4
15	Ab Δ	Lydian	+4 anticipates next sound
15	G mi7	Phrygian	III function
16	F mi7	Dorian	II function
16	Bb13+11	Lydian, b7	+11 required
17	E Δ	Ionian	I function, nat. 4 in previous sound
18	A 13+11	Lydian, b7	+11 required
19	D Δ	Ionian	I function, nat. 4 in previous sound
20	G 13+11	Lydian, b7	+11 required
21	F# Δ	Ionian	I function, nat. 4 in previous sound
21	A 13-9	Half-Whole Dim.	Natural 13 and -9 required
22	C 13-9	Half-Whole Dim.	Natural 13 and -9 required
23	F Δ	Ionian	I function, nat. 4 in previous sound
24	Bb 9+11	Lydian, b7	+11 required

Love At Last

Dan Haerle

Love At Last - Analysis:

Bar	Chord	Chord/Scale	Considerations
1	F Δ	Ionian	I function, nat. 4 in previous sound
2	A 7+5+9	Super Locrian	Altered 5th and 9th required
3	Bb Δ	Ionian	nat. 4 in previous sound
4	A mi7	Phrygian	b2 in previous sound
5	Ab Δ	Lydian	+4 in previous sound
6	Gb Δ	Lydian	+4 in previous sound
7	C Δ	Ionian or Lydian	Personal taste
8	B 7+5+9	Super Locrian	Altered 5th and 9th required
9	Bb 7sus	Mixolydian	Dominant 7th with sus 4
10	E 7+5+9	Super Locrian	Altered 5th and 9th required
11	Ab 7sus	Mixolydian	Dominant 7th with sus 4
12	D 7+5+9	Super Locrian	Altered 5th and 9th required
13	Gb Δ	Lydian	+4 in previous sound
14	F 7+5+9	Super Locrian	Altered 5th and 9th required
15	E Δ	Ionian	I function, nat. 4 in previous sound
16	Eb7+5+9	Super Locrian	Altered 5th and 9th required
17	Ab mi7	Aeolian	I function, nat. 6 in previous sound
18	A 7+11	Lydian, b7	+11 required
19	D Δ	Ionian	I function, nat. 4 in previous sound
20	G 7+11	Lydian, b7	+11 required
21	Db Δ	Lydian	+4 in previous sound
22	C 7+5+9	Super Locrian	Altered 5th and 9th required

Magic Morning

Dan Haerle

Magic Morning - Analysis:

Bar	Chord	Chord/Scale	Considerations
1	E △	Ionian	I function, nat. 4 in previous sound
2	Eb7+5+9	Super Locrian	Altered 5th and 9th required
3	D 9+11	Lydian, b7	+11 required
4	C#7+5+9	Super Locrian	Altered 5th and 9th required
5	F# mi7	Aeolian	I function, nat. 6 in previous sound
7	D# Ø	Locrian	II function
8	G#7+5+9	Super Locrian	Altered 5th and 9th required
9	C# mi7	Aeolian	I function, nat. 6 in previous sound
10	Eb 7+9	Half-Whole Dim.	+9 required
11	Ab △	Ionian	I function, nat. 4 in previous sound
12	Eb 7sus	Mixolydian	Dominant 7th with sus 4
13	Ab △	Ionian	I function, nat. 4 in previous sound
14	Eb 7sus	Mixolydian	Dominant 7th with sus 4
15	G mi7	Dorian	II function
15	C 7	Mixolydian	V function, unaltered
16	F# mi7	Dorian	II function
16	B 7	Mixolydian	V function, unaltered
17	Eb mi7	Dorian	II function
18	Ab 7	Mixolydian	V function, unaltered
19	Db △	Ionian	I function, nat. 4 in previous sound
20	C 7+9	Half-Whole Dim.	+9 required
21	F △	Ionian	I function, nat. 4 in previous sound
22	F# Ø	Locrian	II function
22	B 7+9	Half-Whole Dim.	+9 required
23	G# mi7	Phrygian	III function
23	C# mi7	Aeolian	VI function
24	F# mi7	Dorian	II function
24	B 7	Mixolydian	V function, unaltered
25	E △	Ionian	I function, nat. 4 in previous sound
26	B 7sus	Mixolydian	Dominant 7th with sus 4

Explanation of Analyses

The chord scale choices given in the preceding analyses are not the only possible options in many of the situations. Those choices are intended to supply sounds which meet the expectation of a listener because of the chord symbols, the melodic implications, the functions, or the context in which the chords are found.

An improvisor always has the option to choose scales which are not expected to produce surprises and variety in the music. However, you must have a point of departure before you begin to choose options. In other words, you have to understand the usual before you can choose the unusual. I believe that there is a certain normal sound to any piece that implies definite choices of chord/scales. Observing those choices (such as the ones in the analyses) will always serve the music well. Even though there may be a lack of harmonic tension or excitement, the piece will at least sound "right." The improvisor's personal taste must dictate to what extent he wants to depart from the norm and treat the music in a more unusual way.

Again, the important point is not one of personal taste but one of developing a concept of analysis that leads you to an understanding of the purity, or true nature, of any composition. An improvisor must have the ability to render the true sound of a piece if he so desires.

Appendix II
A Chord/Scale Syllabus ———————————

Part 1 - Scale Groups

Part 2 - Chord Groups

Part 1 - Scale Groups

Major Modes

The seven modes of the C Major scale:

Harmonic Minor Modes

The seven modes of the C Harmonic Minor scale:

1st Mode — C mi △

2nd Mode — D Ø

3rd Mode — Eb △+5

4th Mode — F mi7

5th Mode — G 7-9-13

6th Mode — Ab △+11

7th Mode — B dim7

Ascending Melodic Minor Modes

The seven modes of the C Ascending Melodic Minor scale:

C Melodic Minor	C mi6 or C mi △
D Dorian, b2	D mi7
Eb Lydian Augmented	Eb △+5
Lydian, b7	F 7+11
Mixolydian, b6	G 7-13
Locrian, #2	A Ø9
Super Locrian	B 7+5+9

Harmonic Major Modes

The seven modes of the C Harmonic Major scale:

1st Mode   C △ or
C △+5

2nd Mode   D Ø

3rd Mode   E mi7 or
E 7+9

4th Mode   F mi △

5th Mode   G 13-9

6th Mode   Ab △+5

7th Mode   B dim7

Symmetrical Altered Scales

Chromatic, Whole Tone, Augmented and Diminished scales:

The Chromatic Scale - any chord

Whole Tone Scales - Dominant 9+5

Augmented Scales - Major 7 or Major 7+5

Symmetrical Altered Scales (continued)

Whole-Half Diminished - Diminished 7

Half-Whole Diminished - Dominant 7-9+9

Pentatonic and Blues scales

Pentatonic Scales

Major   C 6 or C 7

Minor   C mi7 or C 7

Blues Scales

Major   C 6 or C 7

Minor   C mi7 or C 7

Exotic scales

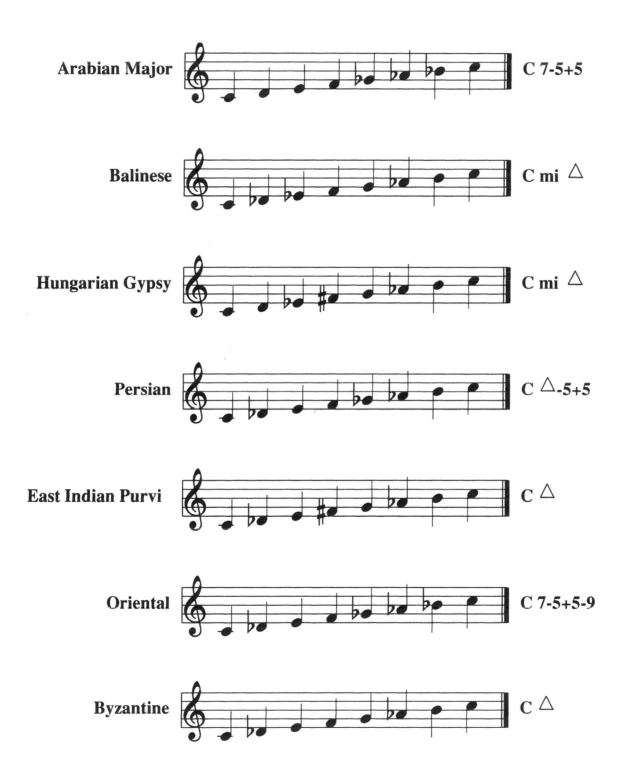

Arabian Major	C 7-5+5
Balinese	C mi △
Hungarian Gypsy	C mi △
Persian	C △-5+5
East Indian Purvi	C △
Oriental	C 7-5+5-9
Byzantine	C △

Part 2 - Chord Groups

Major Chord Group

Chord	Function	Scale	
C 6	Any	Major Pentatonic	
C 6	Any	Major Blues	
C △	I	Ionian	
C △	Any	Augmented	
C △	I	Harmonic Major	
C △+11	IV or I	Lydian	
C △+11	VI	6th Mode Harmonic Minor	

Major Chord Group (continued)

Chord	Function	Scale	
C △+5	Any	Lydian Augmented	
C △+5	Any	Augmented	
C △+5	Any	3rd Mode Harmonic Minor	
C △+5	Any	Harmonic Major	
C △+5	Any	6th Mode Harmonic Major	
C △+5	Any	Synthetic Pentatonic	
C △+5	Any	Synthetic Pentatonic	

Minor Chord Group

Chord	Function	Scale	
C mi6	Any	Ascending Melodic Minor	
C mi6	Any	Synthetic Pentatonic	
C mi6	Any	Synthetic Pentatonic	
C mi6 or 7	I, II or IV	Dorian	
C mi7	I or VI	Aeolian	
C mi7	III	Phrygian	
C mi7	Any	Minor Pentatonic	

Minor Chord Group (continued)

Chord	Function	Scale	
C mi7	IV	4th Mode Harmonic Minor	
C mi7	II	Dorian, b2	
C mi7	Any	3rd Mode Harmonic Major	
C mi7	I	Minor Blues	
C mi △	I	4th Mode Harmonic Major	
C mi △	Any	Ascending Melodic Minor	
C mi △	I	Harmonic Minor	

Dominant 7th Chord Group

Chord	Function	Scale	
C 7 or C 7sus	Any	Mixolydian	
C 13	Any	Bebop Scale	
C 13	Any	Major Pentatonic	
C 7+11	V or IV	Lydian, b7	
C 13sus	Any	Major Pentatonic on the 4th	
C 9sus	Any	Major Pentatonic on the 7th	
C 13+11	Any	Synthetic Pentatonic on the 9th	

Dominant 7th Chord Group (continued)

Chord	Function	Scale	
C 7+5	Any	Whole Tone	
C 7-13	V	Mix., b6	
C 13-9	V	5th Mode Harmonic Major	
C 13-9+11	V	Lydian, b7 b2	
C 13+9 or C 13-9	Any	Half-Whole Diminished	
C 13+9	Any	Major Blues	
C 7+9	Any	Minor Pentatonic	

<u>Dominant 7th Chord Group</u> (continued)

Chord	Function	Scale	
C 7+9+11	Any	Minor Blues	
C 7-9-13	V	5th Mode Harmonic Minor	
C 7 alt.	V	Super Locrian	
C 7 alt.	V	3rd Mode Harmonic Major	
C 7 alt.	Any	Major Pentatonic on b9	
C 7 alt.	Any	Major Pentatonic on b5	
C 7 alt.	Any	Major Pentatonic on #5	

Half-Diminished Chord Group

Chord	Function	Scale	
C Ø	VII or II	Locrian	
C Ø	II	2nd Mode Harmonic Minor	
C Ø9	II	Locrian, #2	
C Ø9	II	2nd Mode Harmonic Major	
C Ø9	II	Synthetic Pentatonic	
C Ø	II	Synthetic Pentatonic	
C Ø	II	Synthetic Pentatonic	

Diminished 7th Chord Group

Chord	Function	Scale	
C dim7	#VII	7th Mode Harmonic Minor	
C dim △	Any	Whole-Half Diminished	
C dim7	#VII	7th Mode Harmonic Major	
C dim7	Any	Synthetic Pentatonic	
C dim7	Any	Synthetic Pentatonic	
C dim7	Any	Synthetic Pentatonic	
C dim △	Any	Synthetic Pentatonic	

Appendix III - Glossary ——————————

Nomenclature:

Item	Common Variations	In This Book
Major 7th	Maj7, Ma7, M7, 7, △	△
Minor 7th	min7, mi7, m7, -7, mi △	mi7, mi △
Dominant 7th	7, b7	7
Half-Diminished	min7-5, mi7 b5, Ø	Ø
Diminished	dim7, di7, d7, °, dim △	dim, dim △
Raised alterations	#5, #9, #11, +5, +9, +11	+5, +9, +11
Lowered alterations	b5, b9, b13, -5, -9, -13	-5, -9, -13
Suspended chord	sus4, sus	sus

General:

A key letter by itself indicates a major triad.

A key letter and a number other than 4 or 6 indicates a dominant family chord, ie. C 7, C 9, C +11, C 13.

A plus sign (+) always indicates a raised chord tone. If a tone is added to the chord, the word "add" is used, ie. add 9.

A minus sign (-) always indicates a lowered chord tone. If a tone is left out of a chord, the word "omit" is used, ie. omit 5.

The word sus without a number is assumed to mean a suspended 4th. Sometimes the suspension may apply to another chord tone, ie. sus 2.

A sharp (#) or a flat (b) in the name of a scale implies a raised or lowered tone. The particular note wouldn't necessarily carry the accidental.

Terms:

Alteration — A chord tone which has been raised or lowered from its normal position by a half step.

Bracketing — Treating two or more chords with the same sound.

Cadence — A progression, usually of two or three chords, which establishes a key.

Chord/Scale — A scale that relates to a chord for improvisation.

Chord Symbol — A combination of key letter, alterations, modifications and extensions of a chord.

Color — A unique combination of chord tones and alterations.

Common Denominator — A tone that is in common with two or more sounds which can serve as a tonal center for comparison.

Context — The position in a progression (between two chords) in which a chord is found.

Cycling — Root movement by 5ths.

Extension — A chord tone found above the basic structure of a 7th chord, ie. the 9th, 11th, or 13th.

Flow — The horizontal motion through the harmony which involves some tones changing and others continuing.

Function — The location of a chord in a major or minor key and the way in which it relates to other chords of the key.

Guide Tones — Tones which serve as anchor points on which to build melodic ideas.

Harmonic — Relating to some aspect of the harmony or a chord.

Improvisation — Using scale and arpeggio motion to create new melodies based on a given harmonic structure.

Modification — A change other than an alteration in a chord, such as sus 4, add 9, etc.

Modulation — Change of key.

Progression — A series of chords which relate to each other.

Tonality — Key area.

Substitution — A chord which can replace another chord because it shares color tones in common and functions the same.

Synthetic — In reference to scales, a structure not commonly found as a mode of a conventional scale.

Vocabulary — In music, melodic patterns and phrases which have been learned and are available to an improvisor.